Let's skip the old comparisons,
like, "Love that's aged to vintage wine."
We've reached a new stage that begins
with words that are uniquely mine.

Love Poems as We Age

A man to his wife in their 60s

By Jeffrey Zygmont

The poem *Keeping Pace* on page 8 was previously published in the book *White Mountain Poems*, by Jeffrey Zygmont, Free People Publishing, 2014.

Cover illustration by Daniel Pantano

ISBN: 978-0-9991163-8-8

Library of Congress Control Number: 2021949126

Printed in the United States of America

Free People Publishing
Salem, New Hampshire
www.freepeepub.com

Love Poems as We Age

CONTENTS

A Note to the Reader:

Although the primary audience for this book is one person, my wife, I also offer it to you and to all the world as a testament to how love matures and flourishes across decades. Please read these forty-five poems for their universal value. Together, they are this poet's reflection on the sturdy and enduring structure built by two partners when they live devotedly and persistently as a pair.

Poetry is an exceptional art to deliver that message because it reaches us through both our brains and our emotions. The idea inside a poem engages our minds and stimulates thought, while at the same time the sound of the poem grabs our aural sense and pleases us.

In metrical poetry like mine, the poet selects words for their sound as well as their meaning, and combines them in deliberate patterns and orders so that the sound of each line and the sound of the poem as a whole carries the poem's message to you, alongside the actual meanings of the words. Therefore please read these poems slowly, to hear them. If you can't read them aloud, form each word in turn in your mind, as if you are privately reciting.

From that I wish you rich reflections of your own.

Jeffrey Zygmont

OUTDOORS

EDEN

I watched you in your survey of our garden:
You walked toward a bed to view a flower,
and paused and lingered in the leafy margin
where lawn gives way to densely planted bower.
And there I saw a scene of harmony,
of you amid the richly growing bounty
of nature represented equally
in you and in the garden, pleasing me.

At Play

This thing you call a garden cart
is just the wagon of a child:
A frame, four wheels, a handle part,
with rack attached where loads are piled.
I watch you wheel it on the lawn
while watering your flower bed
with pails of water freshly drawn,
content with where your duty led,
at labor like a child at play,
as shining as the summer day,
self-absorbed, emitting joy –
your garden cart's a child's toy.

GARDEN VIEW

From our kitchen window
I have a view of you
by looking out onto
the backyard where we grew
so many shrubs and trees,
and raked so many leaves,
and planted little seeds,
and pulled so many weeds,
and separated bulbs,
and pruned those many shrubs,
and fertilized the grass,
and mowed it pass by pass,
and shaped our landscape how
it is a garden now.
The view our window gives
shows how our labor lives
in beauty built by two,
and in that I see you.

Napped Pathway

My wife laid stones
to make a pat-
ee-oh behind
our home, and flags
to make a walk
that leads me to
a shower stall
outside where I
in summer cleanse
myself and feel
the nap of stone
abrade my soles
when I approach
and exit too.
With body clean
my feet enjoy
the gentle scruff.
She anchors my
routine enough.

Beacon

When I drive home to you late in the night,
I find our porch and driveway lights too bright.
You switch them on, I know, to help me see.
But I prefer the lamp more close to thee,
inside the house, which from the window shines
sufficiently because its path aligns
precisely with the light that drew me here:
My urgency to keep you always near.

HOME

The hardwood floor that's just inside the door
we regularly enter, with wet shoes
and sometimes muddy boots from outdoor chores
is blackened now inside the seams and grooves
that lie between the boards, where water seeped
into the grain and stained each edge of wood.
While farther in the flooring boards escaped
the entry's damage and retain the good
close fit and uniform appearance
that are hallmarks of a well-constructed floor.
As if our home denies the outdoor's entrance,
or checks it at one step beyond the door,
and holds us in our private sanctuary
where only we together love and tarry.

Our Dog

I understand our dog is mine.
You'd never have a dog that's thine.
You never cared to have a pet
just for yourself alone. And yet
you recognize my basic need
for dog of undetermined breed,
some common mutt who, as my friend,
will walk with me, and roam, and wend.
You see that I'm no different from
a spunky mutt whose pleasures come
from finding insights that are new
on pathways that are trod by few,
which is just how I want to be,
for which our dog and I thank thee.

KEEPING PACE

You say you hike too slow and warrant me
to step ahead so your obstructing pace
will not impede my brisker strides nor force
me to delay an eager, brusque ascent.
You worry your slow progress will annoy
my high ambition to subdue this peak
and gain its distant summit without pause.
You fear your slower rise will thwart my cause.
But my intention marching here is you.
This mountain hike provides a day's excuse
to linger in your company on trails
that bring this common purpose we now share.
To rush ahead on faster legs denies
my partnered spirit higher victory
achieved ascending patiently with you.
My greatest gain comes when we walk as two.

FLIGHT

Two herons flew together overhead,
arrayed in line, perhaps four feet apart,
or maybe five. Perhaps the first one led,
or maybe it was merely first to start.
I have seen herons flying singlely.
Perhaps this is a family, I thought.
What other explanation can there be
for herons paired and flying closely wrought?
And then I thought of you, as heron winged
and rhythmical aloft in placid flight,
and I inside your slip-stream flying ringed
by trailing air your passage renders light,
as ever in your presence I find ease,
your form a prop, your breath a clearing breeze.

Family

At first I thought it was a toad,
the fledgling robin on the road.
As I approached, the child took flight
awkwardly, just to alight
upon a limb low overhead.
Nearby a parent robin sped
to fly up to the branch beside
the youth, to watchfully abide.

I called up to the wary pair,
You bring me joy by perching there.
I take you for a mom and child.
I see that even creatures wild
are bound by family fealty.
I leave you to your nesting tree
while I continue down the street,
toward my home, my own to meet.

KITCHEN

COFFEE

Each morning when I walk from home,
one hour with our dog to roam,
in solitude and silence deep,
while you are still in bed asleep,
I contemplate some vexing thought,
but afterward am always brought
back to the house I had departed.
Window lights announce you've started
preparations for your day.
I shake the grit of trail away
and enter through our common door,
and step upon our common floor
and smell the brewing coffee scent,
a signal made without intent,
nevertheless assuring me
our kitchen is where I must be.
Or any room inside the home
where you and I reside as one.
Coffee aroma may be small,
but here discerned, it tells me all.

11

Cooking for Two

I am annoyed when you do kitchen work.
You do not put a thing away. It stays
upon the counter top: Utensils lurk
on working surfaces; a wrapper splays
across a space where I would like to chop.
You see, your habits interfere a lot
when I am working close to you. I stop
to wipe a spot, or move a dirty pot
to bring some order to your scattered mess.
It's not that our work habits must align.
I know that your priorities are less
concerned with kitchen order than are mine.
We both contribute culinary gifts.
Perhaps we should just work in separate shifts.

12

But shared tasks are a plain reality.
And cooking can require cooperation,
especially when our whole family
is coming for a special celebration.
And sometimes even when it's just we two,
if preparations for a meal demand
that cooking must be shared by me and you
because some tasks require another hand.
Our purpose then is not just to cohabit.
We are two people closely bound by need
to couple because one is insufficient,
while we together prosper and succeed.
Which is the model of my life with you.
Cook with me still. You can still strew and spill.

Hounding You

You say that I am like a dog
because I smell you cooking,
and lift my nose and smile and wag
and to the stove come looking
to see what you've prepared for me –
what better tribute can there be
than to signal with my senses
how you rouse my bestiality.

At Table

I cook to win your affirmation
of my culinary skill,
and show there is no diminution
of my will to please you still.
You compliment a meal I made,
I feel my spirits lift.
You chew, gratuity is paid.
For both of us, a gift.

BEDROOM

TERRITORY

When I approach you in the night
to warm myself inside our bed,
and scrunch against you, close and tight,
you think I've come to tease instead.

You say I've come to make you cold.
You wince, you flinch, you push me back.
You slide aside, you dodge, you scold.
But I persist in my attack.

Because I need to seize your life
and hold it close to bolster mine.
I grope for my sustaining wife
because I'm whole when we combine.

It is no trespass, joke or hoax.
In bed I slide toward your side
to claim the place I covet most,
the space where both our hearts abide.

Night Music

The rhythmic snorts and puffs at night
from your unconscious breathing
become a source of my delight
when you're beside me sleeping.
I wish that I was sleeping too.
Your snores disturb my slumber.
But since the noises come from you,
I listen and surrender
to breathing that affirms your life.
What finer music could I hear
than snores from my reclining wife
who through the night is warm and near?

Bed Sides

You thrash and push the blanket off,
complaining that you are too hot.
You roll and curl and stretch and toss,
then crowd toward my warmer spot,
where I remain asleep in bed.
You say that now you've grown too cold
and crave my warmer spot instead.
Your trespass might seem over-bold,
but I don't mind your jostling.
It brings you near for me to hold.
To wake me is a minor thing.
I prize you over slumbering.

Bare Essence

I like that you sleep without clothes.
Not that we're in erotic throes
for which I'd like your skin exposed.
I simply like the purity
of unencumbered nudity
while you lie here in bed with me,
no barrier obscuring you,
your essence open, plain and true.

Bare Perceptions

Let's talk about your body now,
the way its shape has aged: a cow
is how you rate its present state.
You carry too much excess weight,
you say. Your forward pieces sag,
your waist expands, your buttocks drag.
Your form that once showed youthful tone,
in age, you say, is overgrown.

But I watch you remove your clothes
when privately you must expose
your body to prepare for bed,
though modestly you turn to shed
your garments, shielding from my view
deficiencies you loudly rue.
But I see no deficiency.
Your naked body pleases me.

I see soft hills obliquely lit
by settled sun. In silhouette
they undulate as tranquil swells
of fervent Earth, with rounded dells
where shadows lie in calm repose,
where energies recline and doze
because their tasks are finished here:
They've honed a landscape without peer.

In you I see the wealth of time
which slowly shaped your form sublime.

The Right Size

You have insisted on a bigger bed
because you'd like some extra room at night.
While I have pled we keep this bed instead
because our nearness seems to me just right.
All right, we'll move one size up, to a queen,
so you escape my wind and perspiration,
while I accept the wider gap between
our bodies with a shrug of mild frustration.
You'll still be just a short arm's-reach away.
And anyway, the bed that brings us near
is not the structure where our bodies lay.
It is the marriage built up year by year,
which is the truest union that we keep,
regardless of the bed on which we sleep.

After Surgery

The surgeon sliced a four-inch-long incision,
disjointed and exposed my thigh-bone top,
sawed off the femur's head and placed revision:
a new hip joint to make my limping stop.
But not until the wound has time to heal,
which leaves me home entrusted to your care.
Now during convalescence here I feel
more drawn to you than formerly aware.
It's not how you dispense my medication,
or help me climbing in or out of bed.
Instead I see your steady dedication
as more apparent now, not newly bred,
the consequence of love you built to last,
with which you bless me now, as in our past.

INTERCOURSE

The autumn night when I rose restlessly,
surrendering to nagging wakefulness,
and bundled to block out October's cold,
I left the room to read and not disturb you
while you still slept.

Returning in an hour or so I found
the air abrasive when I bared myself.
So sliding under bed-covers for warmth,
I closer moved to gain your radiance,
and still you slept.

I spooned against your bare back as I wrapped
an arm around your warm and velvet torso,
and you became my ember and my flame
who drew rekindled pulses from my heart,
while then we slept.

GROWTH

INCREMENTS

I notice now how large this tree has grown,
although it reached here incrementally,
each increment so small when seen alone
its progress was invisible to me.
Till after these accumulated years,
here under the expanded canopy,
where overhead the tree's spread now appears
to be a metaphor for you and me:
How underground its roots embraced the Earth,
while slowly it attained a lofty height,
and steadily its trunk gained sturdy girth,
supporting limbs that splayed to gather light.
Like how I view us two together now:
Aloft, as only years of growth allow.

Discovery

When we were young and life was all a wonder,
and we together marveled as we grew,
and commonplace sensations shook like thunder,
because to us the commonplace was new,
then finding unique qualities in you
was easy, with my eyes so widely opened
to capture and retain each novel view
accumulating richly as we ripened.
Until we both had seen and done so much,
together reaching such a saturation,
we recognized the commonplace as such,
and life became a repeat situation.
How could I find you novel anymore,
when things I saw were things I'd seen before?

But life is not a static enterprise.
It changes as time brings us to new places.
And living well demands we recognize
we must abandon selves that time erases,
and alter to conform to changing roles,
like we'll conform to roles our dotage brings,
like you through time recalibrate your goals
and therefore always show me different things
about yourself, despite proximity.
I see you weep when our grown child moves out.
I watch you bloom to grand-maternity.
I view new grit when job woes twist about.
I learn your lure was never novelty;
I'm drawn to qualities I daily see.

Rerfreshment

I would expect adventure then,
when you and I were new,
and I was just discovering
the novelty of you.

But newness is a fleeting charm.
Soon you grew familiar,
and we proceeded arm in arm,
adventurous no more.

And yet, despite what I expect,
I still see novelty,
arising from how you react
to life lived commonly.

A bright inflection in your voice.
New TV shows you've found.
An unexpected menu choice.
A bird's nest on the ground.

Your worry you may have bad breath.
New musings about Trump.
You humored by a chicken's death.
Ignoring a breast lump.

All show me the fresh turns you take
and fill me with surprise.
By facing life your way you make
adventures in my eyes.

You Address That Fallen Nest

I'm sorry, little song bird,
to see you've lost your nest.
Of all the other nests I've seen,
yours surely is the best.
Of long and silken horse hair,
lost from some horse's tail,
which you spun round to make a cup
of marvelous detail,
of circularly woven strands
and sunken center hollow,
where nestlings could repose in warmth
and comfortably wallow.

Until cruel wind dislodged it,
and hurled it to the ground,
and left your artwork orphaned here,
this treasure I have found.
With gold paint I'll adorn it,
a dusting of a spray,
and keep it as an ornament
and never toss away.
I'll place it within common view
inside my settled home,
where it can be admired alone,
no chance to be wind-blown.

I know that contradicts you.
You didn't make a charm.
You built this nest to house your young
and shelter them from harm.
But nature overruled you
and flung it from the tree,
the same as nature may inflict
some cruelties on me.
In that we are united,
earth-born companions here,
who see our best plans go awry
when powers interfere.

Please rebuild, little song bird,
as lovely as before,
while with your fallen nest I'll prove
there's beauty in the chore
of commonplace survival,
of labors we must do,
embodied in this nest you made
and I preserve for view,
inside the ordered home I'll keep
despite the whims of fate,
and like you, by my efforts reap
true beauty, small but great.

(With gratitude to Robert Burns
  and also *To a Mouse*.)

29

Retention

You are the girl I married long ago,
though you complain how age now makes you slow –
you can't accomplish as much as before –
once-easy tasks now seem a taxing chore.
You say that any effort to lose weight
succumbs to what you place upon your plate –
you can't remember names, events and dates –
you wander sometimes in befuddled states.
But spirit is the essence of existence.
Your spirit shimmers brightly, with persistence.
You may complain of aging's ill effects,
but fundamentally your face reflects
eternal mirth, resilience, inner glow.
You are the girl I married long ago.

Continuity

In youth you knew a spontaneity
of laughter, mirth and instant gaiety.
Your effervescence captured your expression.
Your open face gave laughter full possession.
Your elevating spirit burst outside,
as now, in later age, it cannot hide.
I see it still: It rises in your eyes
and unrestrained your merriment survives
the maturation of some forty years.
It lightens my heart still. Your laughter cheers
my spirit with the joy it radiates.
Infectiously it tickles and elates –
the same delight you brought me in our youth.
Thus nothing's lost, though age now claims us both.

LATE SUMMER SONG

Why must the crickets wait till summer wains?
Why must they remain silent through July,
when green prevails from early summer rains,
and wait instead till August becomes dry,
and summer's end steps plainly into sight,
to then begin their softly sawing rasp,
and give their soothing music to the night,
in songs that signal summer's weakened grasp?
If they chirped earlier, in summer's prime,
their oscillating chime would light the dark
of night at nature's most triumphant time,
when leaves are nappy green and fireflies spark.
But since their music waits till summer's end,
the cricket songs and melancholy blend.

But that is only our association
from our experience of seasons past.
We love the summer so, we feel frustration
when signs arise that show it cannot last.
But hear a cricket song in isolation,
outside the prejudice lodged in our mind,
and it becomes a strum of exaltation,
a tick-tock hymn both joyous and refined.
The same as I observe when seeing you
now even though our season has grown late.
Not yearning for the younger girl I knew,
but viewing beauty in your present state,
I find contentment concentrated here,
as great as any late or early year.

INVESTMENT

I cannot comprehend the wealth
I now possess from life with you,
accruing slowly here with stealth,
compounding greatly as we grew.
These riches now where I reside,
where faithfully you too abide,
come from our presence side by side
increasing what plain fates provide.

My treasure is the complement
created with the wealth you bring.
Your steady love, keen temperament,
determination – everything
that you contribute to create
an entity more richly grown,
creates a life more consummate,
than you or I alone could own.

And so I marvel with surprise
that my exalted state today
exceeds what I could realize
through life the ordinary way.
Your lasting love enriches me
much more than I once thought would be.

DURING LIFE

I do not have at my command,
and can't pretend to understand
what happens to me when I die.
I'll be a spirit in the sky
perhaps, for all eternity
to float in calm serenity
with powers that created me –
if such powers have things so ordained.
My human vision is too far restrained
to see what afterlife will be.

But disregarding afterlife,
in present time you are a wife
who brings me bliss that's heaven-like,
so I presume, when visions strike
that light my eyes with clarity,
which happens intermittently,
but still enough for me to see
that satisfaction I feel here on earth
from love from you is of the highest worth,
which hints what paradise must be.

First Impression

I am thankful for the fact that when I met you
I knew I must keep you forever mine.
I am happy my first observations grew
to firmer certainty I must combine
with you, together our two lives to blend,
in triumphs celebrated as a couple,
in rifts encountered that would slowly mend,
in tragedies when both would clear the rubble.
The qualities I saw in you back then
remain the same sustaining me today.
I have been fortunate to comprehend
you occupy the home where I must stay.
If in my life I have done one thing right,
that thing is knowing that you are my light.

Rebirth

Don't look for me in our old photographs.
I'm not the boy who posed with you so often,
in former time and through that long elapse
while our two lives both grew more closely woven.
My bond with you grew to predominate,
and shaped me to become a different man.
The man you knew was my raw surrogate,
transformed now, when my second life began.
The many times I told you I love you
if heard today would seem to be untrue.
The young and undeveloped love I knew
is nothing now compared to love that grew
from life with you, who made my growth complete,
to whom mature *I love yous* I repeat.

The Plea

Never abandon me
because without you near
my remnant self would see
the closing of the year:
December in a bag,
with daylight at its ebb,
the sky a grayish slag,
all vegetation dead,
the Earth in cold decay,
my life a misery
if you should go away.
Never abandon me.

GIVING

Full Measure

Your father walked you to me as my bride.
I may have got the worse of that exchange.
Your temper sometimes makes me want to hide.
Your ire can peak above derangement range.
Such deep extremes of personality
are evident in other ways as well.
Sometimes you show so much concern for me
your care surrounds me like an ocean swell
and lifts me more than ordinary care.
You send your entire essence to my aid,
and strip your self-regard and ego bare,
since even those are packaged and conveyed
to me, when you defer to how you feel.
I clearly have the better of the deal.

Full Measure Too

There is no measure for my love for you.
Completed things no longer have a scale
from lesser up to greater – nothing new
adds substance once full quantities prevail.
The well that's drilled until fresh water's found
attains its final depth and drilling ends.
The man who finds the home to which he's bound
no longer has a road on which he wends.
My love has grown to full capacity,
first from our early urge to procreate,
through partnership to raise our family,
to when our time together now grows late,
my love has reached the most that love can be,
because you've given all your love to me.

INADEQUACY I

If you should have a next time, don't choose me.
If you return re-incarnated here
to choose again whose loving spouse you'll be,
select a man whose future will not veer
to my pursuit of worthless poetry.
Instead pick one who seeks financial gain,
and therefore brings you more prosperity
than my poetics ever will attain.
No wage is paid, for instance, when I write
how I draw solace from your bed-side light,
how your close breathing comforts me at night,
how your appearance turns my morning bright.
Regretting it's not more, I give my best:
These words through which my love for you's expressed.

Inadequacy II

A poet makes a poor husband, I've shown.
You trudge to your employment every day,
supporting us with what you earn alone,
which makes my labors seem too much like play.
There's no remuneration from a poem.
But making one requires a heaping share
of time in which the poet's thoughts must roam,
plus effort to convey what's hidden there,
which may enrich the public with a view
of life's small truths and beauties seen anew,
like feelings I strive to express to you
about how rich the love between us grew,
which won't put dollars in our joint account,
but which your husband gives in great amount.

Apart Together

You say I'm weird and think I'm comical.
I know I'm not an ordinary guy.
I'm happy that you find hysterical
occasional bon mots that I let fly.
I'm happy that my stubborn oddities,
although they isolate me from most men,
to you are entertaining traits that please
and humor you, and raise me in your ken.
I'm happy to uniquely stand apart
from lifestyles that are commonplace and known,
and with you to pursue my separate art,
because you take my lifestyle as your own,
and find in mine a life with which to blend
your life, as weirdly we together wend.

Valentine Day

What fool says I should take today alone
to give you paper heart, pajama-gram,
red roses, golden necklace, precious stone?
A single day of tribute is a sham.
As if such gestures, made so easily,
accomplished with so little thought and care,
express the weight and fixed enormity
of timeless, settled love that's always there.
I don't care what the advertisers say,
or how much Hallmark Cards wants me to spend.
I won't reduce to just a single day
a love for which there is no start and end.
I'll make each day my valentine to you
with gifts conveyed through everything I do.

FAMILY

HERIARCHY

I tell our dog I love her
and I say the same to you.
I tell our dear grandchildren
and our son and daughter too.
I loved my parents very much.
My siblings know affection.
But I hold you above the bunch
and love you to perfection.

Expansion

You give so much to them that I might think
love's maximum at last has reached its brink,
and you don't have enough still left for me,
your heart already past capacity.
But they all come from us, and we both share
the love for them that motivates your care.
When doting on our offspring you appear
the same to me as when you draw me near.
I feel no discord, envy or regret
because our children and grandchildren get
the full advantage of the love you own.
It is a love we have together grown,
first for ourselves, and then for those who came
as products of our love, we love the same.

Sedimentary Rock

Do you remember in our youth
two children who consumed us both
with hopes and joys and also cares?
Our lives were wholly wrapped with theirs.
We knew no finer lives to live.
We did not hesitate to give
ourselves completely to each child,
while seasons passed and layers piled
beneath, like river sediments,
submerged, but laid with permanence.
They captured and retained the silt
eroding from the lives we built
unconsciously, but as a pair.

And now we float unladed here
alone, our children fully grown.
The sediments below our home
have hardened now to layered stone,
composed of hopes and joys we've known
together, our endowed foundation.
I have no greater expectation
than to remain forever here
with you, who makes my future clear
from what you brought me in the past,
a stream of love from first to last.

REMINDER

The love surprises me sometimes.
Like when this child, who is of us,
one generation from our primes,
was rapt in play and seized me thus:
Too lank and gangly at age nine,
she hopped in clumsy bounds from me.
Then turning, she retraced her line
and ran toward me awkwardly –
with beauty I could hardly bear.
Not from her childish stumbling,
from freshness like the morning air,
from youth out of her tumbling.
She claimed my gaze. She made me stare.
My tears came softly bubbling.

And naturally I thought of you,
through people you begot with me,
our children and grandchildren too,
renewing grand humanity.
A lone child self-absorbed in play
exists because we brought her here,
and stay to nurture her today,
though our demise is creeping near.
She and the others are the gifts
unconsciously each gave to each.
Through warm accords and chilly rifts
we paired for them, to care, to teach.
And now their common presence lifts
my heart and draws you near in reach.

First Will and Testament

We have already given our inheritance
to offspring we begot, brought home and raised.
Our legacy was granted at their entrance,
when we made them the focus of our days.
And nights as well, committing everything
to constructing in them sturdy characters,
that gave them living wealth at their departing
from our home to pursue their own adventures.
In which they are engaged in now, while we
together share a later legacy
bequeathed from early efforts that we made
to give them strength and virtues, now repaid
in settled satisfaction that we know.
We made our children wealthy long ago.

And now we reach the final page,
where this display of words must end.
Let's grow into a later age,
when I'll converse with you again.